I0896298

The Snowbirds are the Canadian Forces' official air display team.

SNOWBIRDS

HIGH FLYERS

JOE TISCHLER

CREATIVE EDUCATION · CREATIVE PAPERBACKS

Published by Creative Education and Creative Paperbacks
P.O. Box 227, Mankato, Minnesota 56002
Creative Education and Creative Paperbacks are imprints of The Creative Company
www.thecreativecompany.us

Book Design by Wyeth Morgan
Art direction by Blue Design (www.bluedes.com)

Images by Getty Images/David Kawai/Bloomberg, 4-5, Terry Moore/Stocktreck Images, 8, 18, 29; Public Domain, 7; Wikimedia Commons/Andrew Rivett, 2, Canadian Department of National Defense, 30, Commons Photographer, 14, Gorgo, 11, John Davies - CYOW Airport Watch, 32, Letartean, 12-13, Mass Communication Specialist 2nd Class James R. Evans/U.S. Navy, 6, Mike, 22, Naomi Gordon, 10, Peter K Burian, 26, Russ, cover, 1

Library of Congress Cataloging-in-Publication Data
Names: Tischler, Joe, author.
Title: Snowbirds / Joe Tischler.
Description: Mankato, Minnesota : Creative Education and Creative Paperbacks, [2026] | Series: High flyers | Includes bibliographical references and index. | Audience: Ages 10-13 | Audience: Grades 4-6 | Summary: "Big diamond. Canada burst. Double take. The Royal Canadian Air Force Snowbirds perform stunning aerobatic displays. Soar high with the Snowbirds in this elegantly designed, visually stunning introduction to their history, present, and future, geared toward upper-elementary readers"— Provided by publisher.
Identifiers: LCCN 2025015370 (print) | LCCN 2025015371 (ebook) | ISBN 9798895810668 (library binding) | ISBN 9798896800194 (paperback) | ISBN 9798895811924 (ebook)
Subjects: LCSH: Canada. Canadian Armed Forces. Snowbirds--Juvenile literature. | Stunt flying—Canada—Juvenile literature. | Aeronautics, Military—Canada—Juvenile literature. | Air shows—Canada—Juvenile literature. | CYAC: Stunt flying. | Military aeronautics. | Air shows.
Classification: LCC UG632.3.C2 T57 2026 (print) | LCC UG632.3.C2 (ebook) | DDC 797.5/40971—dc23/eng/20250512
LC record available at https://lccn.loc.gov/2025015370
LC ebook record available at https://lccn.loc.gov/2025015371

Printed in the United States

ABOUT THE AUTHOR — Joe Tischler lives in Minnesota with his wife Gwen, son Toby, and dog Meg. He enjoyed attending airshows as a kid and continues to admire the bravery of the men and women of flight teams who put on air demonstrations for the viewing public.

The Snowbirds perform with nine aircraft.

CONTENTS

WING TIPS

The Snowbirds fly in tight formations, with wingtip overlaps as close as 4 feet (1.2 meters). ↗

HIGH FLYERS

Snowbirds in Flight

Nine planes are flying in formation in the clear, blue skies. Their red and white underbellies sport the colors of their country, Canada. Officially called the 431 Air Demonstration Squadron, the Snowbirds show off their flying skills to a U.S. audience in Oshkosh, Wisconsin.

The planes are CT-114 Tutors. Together, they seem to form a single giant plane. At speeds of up to 370 miles (595.5 kilometers) per hour, the planes are just feet (meters) apart! Some have smoke outputs so the crowd can see the shapes they make.

Later in the show, four planes work in a formation. Two of them veer off to the left while two glide to the right. They are working to form an object with the smoke trails. At the end of the routine, fans can see a heart. Music from the movie *Top Gun: Maverick* plays in the background.

The nine planes reunite to perform one final maneuver. They nosedive until they get close to the ground, then level up and fly off in different directions. The crowd roars in approval of the high-flying acrobatics.

HOW THE SNOWBIRDS GOT THEIR NAME

The flight team began in 1971 as the Snowbirds. In 1978, it was renamed officially as 431 Air Demonstration Squadron. But it is still known worldwide as the Snowbirds. The team is based in the city of Moose Jaw, in the Canadian province of Saskatchewan. A "Name the Team" contest was held at the local elementary school on the base. A sixth grader named Doug Farmer submitted the winning entry. The name reflected the aircraft's mostly white paint scheme at the time. Snowbirds stood for grace and beauty and linked to the team's Canadian origins.

The Snowbirds' name reflects pride in their country.

The Snowbirds often perform flybys at national events like Canada Day celebrations and military ceremonies.

A Canadian pilot stands in front of a CT-114 Tutor jet, 1987.

HIGH FLYERS

Air Display History

The Snowbirds formed in 1971. They are the aerobatic flight demonstration team of the Royal Canadian Air Force (RCAF). But Canadian flight demonstration teams have been around for more than 100 years. The first known aerial formation demonstration in Canada took place at the Canadian National Exhibition (CNE) in Toronto, Ontario, in 1919. It was led by Lieutenant Colonel William G. Barker. He was a decorated fighter ace from World War I (1914–18). He and three other veterans from the war flew daily performances at the CNE.

The RCAF was formed in 1924. It is responsible for all aircraft operations of the Canadian Forces. It enforces the security of Canada's airspace and provides aircraft to support the missions of the Royal Canadian Navy and the Canadian Army. In 1929, Canada's first official aerobatic team was formed. It was called the Siskins. They flew for four seasons. The Siskins were followed by a variety of teams across Canada, as well as the RCAF's 1 Air Division in Europe. Teams included the Blue Devils, Easy Aces, Prairie Pacific, Sky Lancers, Grey Ghosts, and the Red Knight.

The RCAF Golden Hawks started in 1959 to celebrate the 35th anniversary of the RCAF and the 50th anniversary of powered flight in Canada. The team flew more than 300 public air displays over five seasons. Government budget cuts plagued the team. They were forced to disband in 1964. The Golden Hawks gained much publicity and good will across North America, which led to the formation of a new team in 1967. They were called the Golden Centennaires because 1967 was Canada's 100th year as an independent country. A 100th anniversary is called a centenary.

The Centennaires had a team of eight Canadair CT-114 Tutor jet trainers. The squad featured six-plane formations taking turns with two solo aircraft. The team

CANADIAN HALL OF FAME FLYER

Owen Bartley "O. B." Philp was born to be a flyer. His father, Bart, flew for Canada with the Royal Air Force in World War I. Bart was also a ferry pilot for the RCAF in World War II (1939–45). At just 19 years old, O. B. enlisted in the RCAF during World War II. After years of service, O. B. was chosen to organize the Golden Centennaires aerobatic team. He found the Tutor aircraft used by the Centennaires could be used to form a new aerobatic team and guided a new group of pilots in perfecting airborne maneuvers. This group became the Snowbirds. O. B. was inducted into the Canadian Aviation Hall of Fame in 2015.

set a single-season record for most shows performed in their first year. They flew in 100 public demonstrations in Canada and another eight in the United States.

The 1967 season was the only year the Golden Centennaires flew. Despite the team breaking up, many Canadians wanted a permanent military aerobatic team. One was the Centennaires' commanding officer, Wing Commander O. B. Philp. He was base commander of Canadian Forces Base Moose Jaw, Canada's largest flying training base and home of the Air Force's entire Tutor fleet.

By 1971, Philp had established an unofficial seven-plane formation team, using the Centennaires' Tutor aircraft. On July 11 that year, North America's largest one-day airshow took place in Moose Jaw. The new team was the main attraction. The Snowbirds performed in two other airshows that year. They received positive reviews. This started a new era in Canadian military aerobatics.

The Snowbirds fly more than 40,000 miles (64,373.8 kilometers) every year.

TRAVELING ACROSS NORTH AMERICA

On average, the Snowbirds perform in approximately 60 airshows each season in 40 different cities across Canada and the United States. Their season runs from May through October. As of 2025, they have flown in more than 2,800 official airshows to millions of spectators. They have performed at every major event in Canada. These include the Olympic Games, the Commonwealth Games, the Grey Cup (championship game of the Canadian Football League), and Canada Day celebrations every year in the capital city of Ottawa. The Snowbirds have also flown at every major airshow in Canada and the United States. The top airshows in the United States include the EAA AirVenture in Oshkosh, Wisconsin, and the Sun 'n' Fun Aerospace Expo in Lakeland, Florida.

HIGH FLYERS

Who Are the Snowbirds?

The Snowbirds history is linked to that of the 431 Squadron. Forty-four Canadian squadrons were formed and sent to Europe to help aid in war efforts during World War II. The 431 Squadron was one of them. Their nickname was the Iroquois. It went with their motto, "Warriors of the air." The squadron formed in 1942. They earned 11 battle honors before disbanding after the war in September 1945.

The 431, now called the "Fighter" Squadron, re-formed in January 1954 on a temporary basis. Its duties included aerial combat training and displaying the capabilities of jets to the public at airshows. The unit disbanded that October.

The Snowbirds were officially authorized as the Canadian Forces Air Demonstration Team in January 1975. The Canadian military reactivated the 431 Squadron in 1978. The Snowbirds were officially named the "431 Air Demonstration Squadron."

Fame and success came quickly for the Snowbirds. But like previous Canadian air demonstrations teams, funding was an issue. The Snowbirds were working on a tight military budget. Unlike the previous teams, they were a strong force in the community. Aside from entertaining crowds with their high-flying displays, they held post-show autograph sessions, visited schools and hospitals, and took part in a wide range of social activities with the public. Demand grew for more Snowbirds appearances.

The Snowbirds are made up of about 80 full-time people. Twenty-four are on the show team. They include 11 pilots (9 demonstration pilots, plus 2 "spare" pilots with other duties), technicians, and support staff. All are members of the Canadian Forces (RCAF, Royal Canadian Navy, Canadian Army). They have applied to be on the team. Technicians are chosen based on skills and experience. Pilots must pass a series of rigorous flying tests.

DEMONSTRATION DANGERS

Although airshows can be exciting to watch, they can come with dangers. The Snowbirds have been involved in several accidents since their start in 1971. Seven pilots and two passengers have sadly died during training or performance flights. The first fatality happened in 1972 after a wingtip collision with another aircraft. The most common fatality is a midair crash. Some deaths have occurred due to plane malfunctions. The only time two fatalities occurred was in 2008 when a new pilot traveling with a military photographer crashed while on a non-exhibition flight.

Each season, one-third of the Snowbird team changes. This is done to maintain a uniform level of skill from year to year. Pilots are invited to participate in flying tryouts each fall at the team's base in Moose Jaw. Three are selected to fill vacant flying positions. The tour of duty for each pilot is three years. The Snowbird team lead is called Boss. There is no backup Boss. If Boss cannot fly, the show is canceled. Maintenance members can stay on the team for several years. A ground crew works hard to keep the team's aircraft in working order.

The Snowbird training season starts right after tryouts are completed in late November. Training ends in mid-April. That is done in Comox, British Columbia. Each of the nine demonstration pilots take part in at least 120 practice sessions by the end of training. Then the show season starts. It is a constant routine of traveling, practices, and shows for six months across Canada and the United States.

The red and white jets are a symbol of Canadian pride and aviation excellence.

HIGH FLYERS

Formations

The Snowbird show has grown since its start in 1971. It began with seven aircraft flying in only non-aerobatic maneuvers, or flybys. The following year, two solo aircraft were added. They performed head-on aerobatics. In 1973, the formation was allowed to perform aerobatic maneuvers. It has now grown into one of the most exciting aerial displays in the world.

In 1974, the team adopted its familiar red, white, and blue color scheme. The red and white are the colors of the Canadian flag. The blue stripe along the side of the planes is a tribute to the Golden Centennaires. The bottom of the Centennaires' planes was painted blue.

The team designs formations and maneuvers each season. These must be approved by three organizations: the Canadian

Forces, Transport Canada, and U.S. Federal Aviation Administration (FAA). FAA approval is needed because the team performs shows in the United States. All show maneuvers must be safe for both the team members and the audience.

A Snowbird show involves a complex series of formations and maneuvers. Three shows are designed: a high show when the weather is ideal, a low show, and a flat show. A non-aerobatic show, is also flown.

The maneuvers are traced in smoke so the audience can follow the patterns. Underneath the planes are two fuel tanks which contain diesel fuel. There is a tube from each tank to the exhaust at the back of the engine. The pilot squeezes a trigger to start the flow of diesel from the tank to the engine exhaust. When the diesel fuel enters the exhaust, it turns into vapor and creates a white smoke trail.

WOMEN IN THE SNOWBIRDS

It took 10 years before the first woman served on the Snowbirds. Lieutenant Heather Campbell was the first woman to serve on the team. She was the Snowbirds' executive officer in 1981–82. The first female technician to join the team was Corporal Marline Shillingford in 1993–94. She later returned to be crew chief in 2007. The first, and so far only, woman to fly for the Snowbirds was Captain Maryse Carmichael. She flew as Snowbird Number 3 in 2001 and as Snowbird Number 2 in 2002. She later returned to the squad as commanding officer from 2010 to 2012.

Although new formations and maneuvers are designed each season, some show elements are passed down from one season to another. The main elements include formations such as the Canada Burst, Heart, Downward Bomb Burst, Solo Head-On Crosses, and a signature Nine-Abreast exit. The Snowbirds training consists of more than 50 different formations and maneuvers. These include nine-plane formations, seven-plane formations, and one that is five planes across in a straight line. Some of the nine-plane formations include the Arrowhead, the Big Diamond, the Shuttle, and the Eagle. Some of the seven-plane formations include the Cross, the Double Diamond, the Goose, and the Feather. The Snowbirds were the first aerobatic team in the world to use music in their shows. Music is often used with live commentary from the performing pilots.

Each pilot has amazing hand, eye, and foot coordination. It helps the pilot maintain their relative position within a few feet (meters) of the aircraft behind, in front of, or beside them. The planes fly as close as 4 feet (1.2 m) apart. Their speeds range from 115 miles (185 km) per hour to 370 miles (595.4 km) per hour. Snowbird pilots use nose-down flying techniques when performing difficult maneuvers, especially when they experience turbulence.

Each Snowbird show lasts about 35 minutes. The opener is about 12 minutes long and usually involves two or three loops or rolls in the nine-plane formation. Between the rolls is a top or a bottom side pass. The end of the routine involves more loops.

Each Snowbird aircraft has a pilot and a passenger, with the pilot executing maneuvers and stunts.

HIGH FLYERS

How to Become a Snowbird

The basic Snowbird formation is called the Big Diamond. All nine planes fly in a diamond shape. The pilots have numbers that relate to their positions in the Big Diamond. Boss is Snowbird Number 1. They lead the Big Diamond and all other formations. They also call all formation changes and maneuvers to other pilots on a radio.

Planes Numbers 2 and 3, known as the inner wingers, fly on the left and right sides of Boss. Directly behind Boss are planes Numbers 4 and 5. Plane Number 6 flies behind Number 2, while Number 7 flies behind Number 3. These planes are the outer wingers. On the far left and right sides of the Big Diamond formation are planes 8 and 9, known as the solos. One of these solo pilots, the lead solo, is responsible for giving commands for solo maneuvers. The solos perform aerobatics close to the ground.

To become a Snowbird, one must be a member of the Canadian Forces. To become a Snowbird pilot, one must have at least 1,300 hours of military jet experience. Commanding officers in the Canadian Forces recommend pilots for the Snowbirds. The team then invites six candidates to demonstrate their flying abilities at the Snowbirds base in Moose Jaw. The candidates stay at the base around seven weeks.

Current Snowbird pilots choose the new pilots. They are mainly chosen for their ability to fly in formation. Each candidate's personality is also considered. The previous Boss and Air Force officials select the next Boss. This pilot must have flown previously on the Snowbird team and hold the rank of major.

To become a Snowbird technician, one needs to have experience working on CT-114 Tutors. Commanding officers recommend technicians for the Snowbirds.

↗ **The team's pilots are highly skilled Royal Canadian Air Force members.**

Snowbirds pilots in 1971

MOTHER OF THE SNOWBIRDS

Lois Boyle was a part of the Snowbirds before they officially became a flight demonstration team. She was an administrative assistant to Colonel O. B. Philp. Even though she was not a pilot, she mentored student pilots. She became known as the "Mother of the Snowbirds." She also coordinated the naming of the team contest that came up with the name "Snowbirds." Boyle died in 2012. Her obituary said that Philp told her that the Snowbirds would not have happened without her help. The Lois Boyle Excellence in Community Service Award is handed out every year in Moose Jaw. The award is named after Boyle because she loved the city of Moose Jaw and the Snowbirds base.

The Snowbirds wow crowds in Canada and the United States with their aerial acrobatics. Fans hope they will continue to entertain for many years to come.

The Boss and crew chief then choose skilled candidates with excellent performance records. The technicians fly with the Snowbird pilots to each airshow. They make sure the planes are operating properly.

The CT-114 Tutors have been flying for a very long time. They need upgrades. The Canadian government had plans to replace the Tutors with new aircraft between 2026 and 2035. But it changed its mind and decided to extend the use of the Tutors to 2030. The Tutors will receive modern equipment to comply with regulations and allow the Snowbirds to continue flying in North America. The Tutors' escape system, which includes parachutes and harnesses, will also be upgraded.

Canadian leaders remained concerned that the Tutor has aged out. They were also concerned about safety issues. The Canadian government has asked the RCAF to start searching for a possible replacement aircraft.

The Snowbirds wow crowds in Canada and the United States with their aerial acrobatics. They have been doing so for more than 50 years. Fans hope they will continue to entertain for many years to come.

INDEX

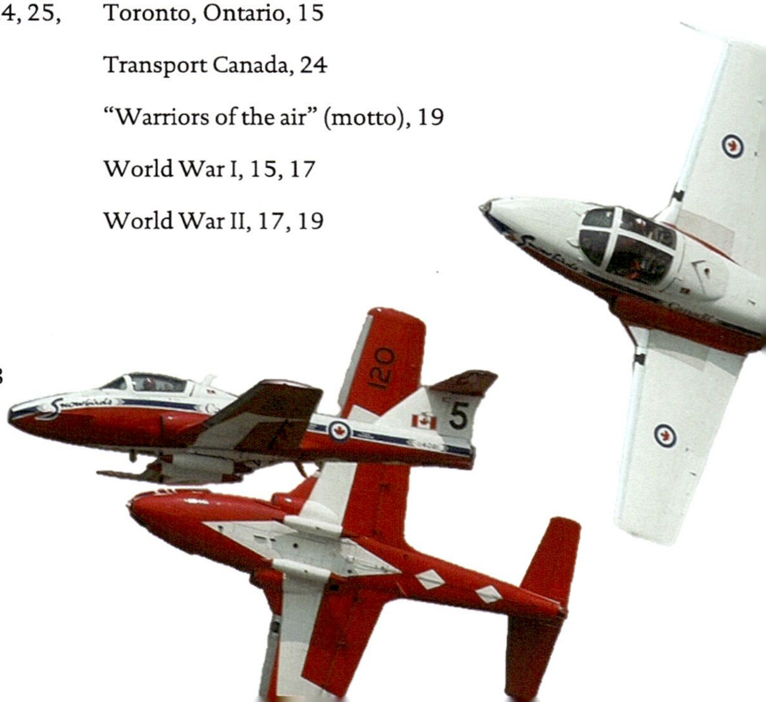